To Diana:
Enjoy!

Bobbi Olson

Marking Time

NEBRASKA'S
HISTORIC PLACES

MARKING TIME

NEBRASKA'S
HISTORIC PLACES

By BOBBI & STEVE OLSON
With text by DAVID L. BRISTOW

NEBRASKA
LIFE

The Sidney-Deadwood Stagecoach at Fort Robinson

CONTENTS

Above: Reenactors bring an 1846 trading post to life at the Museum of the Fur Trade in Chadron.
Right: Tall cottonwoods in Arthur County would surprise pioneers who thought the Sandhills a desert.
Page 1: Fort Niobrara in Cherry County. Page 2-3: The Sidney-Deadwood Stagecoach at Fort Robinson.

Along Whitman Road in Arthur County

Town square gazebo in Broken Bow

"The Great Smoke" near Morrill

MARKING TIME
NEBRASKA'S HISTORIC PLACES

THIS BOOK IS BUILT AROUND A SIMPLE IDEA. It's based on historical markers – those metal signs around the state that tell you that in such-and-such a year, some noteworthy thing happened near this spot.

But it isn't a book of historical photos… and contains few photos of historical markers, and with little text copied from historical markers.

But it's all based on historical markers. Get it?

When husband and wife photographers Steve and Bobbi Olson came to the *Nebraska Life Magazine* office in Norfolk to pitch this book idea – this book-about-historical-markers-except-there's-no-historical-markers – it made perfect sense to us.

To explain, let's say you're driving along Highway 26 just outside Scottsbluff. You see a little blue sign along the road and, on a whim, turn off onto a graveled parking area between the highway and the railroad tracks. The sun is bright and scorching, and there is no wind. Nearby, water gurgles from an irrigation ditch. The tawny bulk of Scotts Bluff National Monument stands like a wall to the west.

Near the little graveled lot is a grave, and beside the grave is metal sign telling the story of Rebecca Winters, buried here in 1852. She and her family were on their way to the Mormon settlements of Utah, but she died here of cholera. Her family buried her, scrawled "Rebecca Winters, Age 50" on an iron wagon tire, and stuck that in the ground as her headstone (it's still here). Then the wagon train moved on.

And so will you, in just a few minutes. And when you do,

Above: "The Great Smoke." Near Morrill in westernmost Nebraska, 8,000 to 12,000 Indians gathered in 1851 to negotiate what became known as the Horse Creek Treaty. Left: Not far from Broken Bow's town square gazebo, the Custer County Museum displays a fragment of the bow for which the town was named.

Fort Robinson State Historical Park

not one physical thing will have changed in the landscape, but it will be different somehow to you. As you continue on through the North Platte Valley, with its lush irrigated fields of wheat and sugar beats, its ragged bluffs, its cottonwood-lined river, you'll think about those people who came this way before you, and what it was like for them, and what they were thinking while they were here.

THAT'S WHAT THIS BOOK IS ABOUT. It's about looking at a place differently, and how you can start to do that as soon as you know just a little of a location's back story. Even the most beautiful landscape gains something as the deep, hidden layers of its past – the boomtowns and pioneer dreams, the crimes and disasters, the edifices and institutions – are revealed.

There are many ways to start looking deeply at the places of Nebraska. You can read books or magazines, talk to old-timers, stop in at a county museum. Sometimes it's as simple as pulling off the road and reading a sign.

So far, more than 400 historical markers have been placed across Nebraska. Together they form a history book of sorts, though not a comprehensive one. Over the years, they've been placed as local groups have raised money for them; each therefore reflects a community's belief about which aspects of the past are worthy of remembrance. Likewise, though all markers must be approved by the Nebraska State Historical Society, each reflects the historical knowledge that existed at the time it was placed. Though the markers inspired this collection, other sources were consulted during the writing. It's something you learn along the way – no guide is perfect, and there's always more to discover.

The book's four chapters represent four overlapping eras, so that page by page the narrative moves more-or-less chronologically from the distant past to the 20th century. But like the markers themselves, this work isn't comprehensive.

Above: Fort Robinson was a frontier outpost when Crazy Horse was murdered here in 1877. Cheyenne captives made a desperate escape a few years later. The fort later became the world's largest military remount depot. Right: The Thayer County Courthouse has been a Hebron landmark since 1903. Page 10-11: In 1864, Indian raids in Nebraska closed the Oregon Trail two months. The worst attacks were along the Little Blue River in Nuckolls County, where about 100 people were killed. Page 12-13: Prairie plants and grasses still flourish along roadsides and fences in Otoe County and across Nebraska.

Thayer County Courthouse

It's a selection of recent photos inspired by a selection of historic sites. Even after years of traveling the state, Bobbi and Steve still feel that they're only beginning to explore Nebraska. If something in these pages inspires you to do a little exploring yourself, we'll all count the project a success.

IN HER BOOK, *Lakota Woman*, Mary Crow Dog writes, "The Sioux used to keep winter counts, picture writings on buffalo skin, which told our people's story from year to year. Well, the whole country is one vast winter count. You can't walk a mile without coming to some family's sacred vision hill, to an ancient Sun Dance circle, an old battleground, a place where something worth remembering happened."

A sacred hill... or a country church. A ghost town... or traces of an earth lodge village. A stone arrowhead... or a rusting horse-drawn plow. It's all part of our vast winter count.

Much has been lost. Pioneers generally placed little value on the accumulated knowledge of those who lived on this land before they did. To prevent similar treatment from generations to come, pioneers and their descendants built museums and erected markers. In a youthful, disposable society, they achieved limited success.

But much has also been restored. Lost sites have been excavated or rebuilt; old stories have been rediscovered and re-told. The winter count keeps changing as people and events pass into and out of historical consciousness. It lives under constant threat from ignorance and indifference – but still it endures in a variety of forms.

You too can find entry points into the past. In your travels, one of the most rewarding discoveries you can make is to learn how to enter two landscapes at once – one of present-day beauty, one of collective memory. 🦅

Page 14-15: Lewis and Clark found this Dixon County bluff hot to the touch; for years after, fur traders often noticed fire and smoke. The "Ionia Volcano" was actually caused by a chemical reaction with minerals. It has since eroded into the river. Page 16-17: A longhorn bull relaxes near Courthouse and Jail Rocks. Page 18-19: In 1804, Lewis and Clark camped near here in present-day Boyd County. Page 20-21: Sandhill crane migration on Platte River, Hall County. Page 22-23: Much of the original Omaha City townsite is now Heartland of America Park.

Little Blue River, Nuckolls County

Near Douglas, Otoe County

The view from Ionia Volcano, Dixon County

Longhorn bull in Morrill County

Real-life cowboys, Boyd County

Sandhill crane migration on Platte River, Hall County

Heartland of America Park, Omaha

Lewis and Clark Lake, Cedar County

Mule Deer, Custer County

WILD NEBRASKA

Settlement and agriculture have transformed Nebraska, but there are still places where nature is closer to the surface. If you look, you'll encounter landscapes reminiscent of those known to our predecessors for thousands of years.

THE PAWNEE SPOKE OF GIANTS. They stood as tall as trees, and grew so proud that God was sorry he'd ever made them. The Pawnee knew this because from time to time they'd find the giants' bones sticking out of the ground in the Republican River valley. That was how they knew of the great flood.

Long before settlers came, the Pawnee were planting corn and hunting bison in the place we call Nebraska. They were here before the other Natives American peoples we now associate with the region, and they may be descendants of people who were living in the Republican valley nearly a thousand years ago.

The Pawnee were aware that others came before them… even if they were mistaken about the identity of the giants' bones. What they found, apparently, were mammoth bones. Mammoths roamed North America during the most recent ice age. They were still here when the first humans arrived in Nebraska.

People have lived in the place we call Nebraska for millennia. What we often think of as the history of the place is really just the topmost layer of a much larger story. For most of that story, the land retained a wild appearance.

Mule deer near Broken Bow. Because of its lack of trees, this was once the heart of the "sod house frontier." Left: Lewis and Clark would recognize the cliffs but not the reservoir. They camped nearby, and mistook sand ridges and mounds left by Missouri River floods for ancient fortifications.

River Origins

We don't know the story of the arrival of Nebraska's original inhabitants. Our tales of discovery come from explorers and pioneers of more recent times. Usually what they encountered first was the Missouri River.

Once upon a time, the ancestral Missouri flowed north from Montana to Hudson Bay. Glaciers have advanced and retreated several times since then. From Montana to Kansas City, the river's present course shows where the edge of a glacier used to be.

Nineteenth-century boatmen called it the "Big Muddy," a name that was also applied to the Mississippi River. But it was the Missouri that gave the Mississippi most of its muddiness. We often think of big rivers as serene, but there was always something about the Missouri that explorers perceived as malevolence.

"Almost every island and sand-bar is covered with huge piles of these floating trees," artist George Catlin wrote in 1841, "and when the river is flooded, its surface is almost literally covered with floating raft and drift wood which bid positive defiance to keel-boats and steamers on their way up the river.

"With what propriety this 'Hell of waters' might be denominated the 'River Styx,' I will not undertake to decide; but nothing could be more appropriate or innocent than to call it the River *of Sticks.*"

That was the beauty of the Missouri. With its shifting channel, its rapidly-eroding banks, its tremendous ice-dams in winter and thunderous breakup in spring, its deadly floods… it wasn't merely big, but was prone to lavish displays of its power over (and indifference to) human affairs. As with all natural things, the river's greatness brought an element of danger.

North Loup River, Blaine County

Today, the river is mostly tamed – dammed, dredged and rip-rapped. It is straighter, narrower and deeper than it was in the old days, and less prone to flooding. And yet some of its old wildness remains. Places like Indian Cave State Park in southeastern Nebraska, Fontenelle Forest in Bellevue, or Ponca State Park in the state's northeastern bend, reveal that the Missouri valley is an ecological corridor of Eastern hardwood forest. Plants and animals not native to the prairies have followed the river valley.

Between Yankton and Ponca State Park, the river itself remains in a wilder state. Just beyond the heavily-wooded bluffs on the Nebraska side, the valley is divided by braided channels and islands. Sandbars are home to endangered piping plovers and least terns, and tall cottonwoods bear the swollen hulks of bald eagle nests. In the water, sudden shoals and hidden "deadheads" (fallen trees) await the careless boatman. Catlin would feel at home.

THE ENDLESS PRAIRIE

Coming from the East, travelers tended to see the prairie in terms of what it lacked. The immensity of land and sky was frightening.

"There seemed to be nothing to see; no fences, no creeks or trees, no hills or fields," writes Willa Cather in *My Ántonia*. "If there was a road, I could not make it out in the faint starlight. There was nothing but land: not a country at all, but the material out of which countries are made."

Like her character Jim Burden (who is the speaker in the passage quoted above), Cather came to Nebraska from Virginia as a child. As Burden says,

"I had never before looked up at the sky when there was not a familiar mountain ridge against it. But this was the complete dome of heaven, all there was of it… Between that earth and that sky I felt erased, blotted out. I did not say my prayers that night: here, I felt, what would be would be."

What settlers perceived as emptiness was actually a place of incredible complexity. Over the years, researchers have found more than 290 species of plants at Nine-Mile Prairie near Lincoln, one of the largest remaining tracts of tallgrass prairie in eastern Nebraska. The grasses and forbs are adapted to withstand harsh winters and drought, and recover quickly after wildfires.

Of the tallgrass prairie (which extends through the eastern quarter of Nebraska), less than five percent remains unplowed. Further west, only about half of the mixed and shortgrass prairies remain. Much of this is in the Sandhills.

Covering a quarter of Nebraska, the Sandhills are the largest region of sand dunes in the western hemisphere. The area is comparable in size to West Virginia. And yet the hills are relatively new. The Sandhills region was probably formed hundreds of thousands of years ago, blown in from the eroding Rocky Mountains – but most of the dunes we see today are less than 15,000 years old.

And some are less than a thousand years old. Sometimes, during decades-long droughts, the hills blow as free as the dunes of the Sahara. This happened most recently during medieval times, and it will probably happen again. Scientists warn that global warming will make this more likely in the future.

Settlers didn't know how the hills were formed; they only knew that the place looked inhospitable. In 1877, a man named E.S. Newman started a ranch along the Niobrara River in Sheridan County, at the edge of the Sandhills. Two years later, he and his men entered the Sandhills to look for cattle that had strayed there during a hard winter. He hoped to salvage at least some of the herd. To his surprise, the cattle had found shelter in the hills, and adequate grass and water. That year, former Army scout Frank North made a similar discovery – which he and his business partner, "Buffalo Bill" Cody, soon capitalized on.

There was a lesson here. Across central Nebraska, other ranchers began discovering that the place they had considered an uninhabitable desert made good cattle country. It still is.

PLATTE RIVER

You could say that the Platte is the most Nebraskan of rivers. It crosses the entire state from west to east. Its broad valley is a natural highway that was traveled by some half a million emigrants during the mid-1800s. It lured the builders of the first transcontinental railroad, and its waters irrigate much of the state.

Even the river's name is Nebraskan. Literally. In 1714, a report by a French trader contained the first written reference to the river "Nibraskier." It was an Otoe word meaning "flat water." In time, the French word for flat, *platte*, replaced it.

The Platte isn't the river it once was. Much of its water is diverted for agriculture, often leaving the riverbed dry in places. The remaining water has for years been polluted with pesticides, fertilizers and animal waste. Naturalist Paul Johnsgard calls it a "ghost of a river."

Still, there's great beauty to be found on the Platte. It is a river worth loving and worth protecting.

It is the Platte, after all (along with the nearby Rainwater Basin), that draws the cranes. From late February to early April, the river is home to as many as 500,000 sandhill cranes, plus a handful of endangered whooping cranes and about 10 million (give or take a few) migrating ducks and geese.

Though the name "sandhill crane" refers to sandhills of the arctic tundra and not to Nebraska's grass-covered dunes, the birds are associated with Nebraska in a unique way. Every spring, 80 percent of the species converges on the Platte Valley as a resting place on the way to their arctic nesting grounds.

THE WESTERN ESCARPMENTS

Coming to western Nebraska after months of travel, Oregon Trail emigrants at last saw Courthouse and Jail Rocks, Chimney Rock and Scotts Bluff in the distance. They knew the Rocky Mountains couldn't be far away.

Flatlanders tend to have a limited vocabulary for steep terrain. Naturalists use the word "escarpment" to describe the Wildcat Hills of the central Panhandle and the Pine Ridge country of the northern Panhandle. The word describes a cliff or steep slope that separates two more-or-less level surfaces. It can result from a fault or from erosion.

Both Nebraska escarpments are the result of erosion. You can see this for yourself by entering the Wildcat Hills from the south or the Pine Ridge from the west. In both cases, the plain falls away suddenly into a broad valley. Standing at the edge of either valley, you'll see the tops of the buttes at slightly below eye level. That's because they've been carved by water and wind from what used to be nothing more than the ground below some prehistoric creature's feet. Their layer-cake appearance shows how the ground was built up gradually, layer upon layer of sediment, over tens of millions of years.

It was probably inevitable that high places like these should acquire legends and stories. To cite but one example among many, a butte called Lover's Leap inspired a tale about two Indian lovers from enemy tribes who leapt to their deaths from the peak. Though it sounds like Shakespeare, settlers insisted it was an Indian legend. But they were right that such a tale is worthy of these buttes. 🐦

Nebraska's name means "flat water," but whitewater can be found along the Niobrara. Upstream from Norden Chute, shown here, Fort Niobrara was built near Valentine to protect settlers from Lakota Indians. Page 26-27: Like the Platte today or the Missouri River of old, the North Loup River's meandering channel carves sandbars and sharp cutbanks.

Norden Chute on the Niobrara River, border of Keya Paha and Brown counties

Missouri River

ALONG THE "BIG MUDDY" Artists and riverboat captains celebrate the connection people still feel to the great river. Above: At Ponca State Park, the "Towers in Time" by Nebraskans Jay and Dean Tschetter represent the long animal and human past along this portion of the river. Right: The Belle of Brownville still tours the river near the town that is its namesake. The formerly snag- and sandbar-filled Missouri was once a terror to steamboatmen. Page 30-31: The Missouri, still a majestic river, is narrower and straighter than it once was.

Belle of Brownville, on the Missouri at Brownville Bridge

Nine Mile Prairie, near Lincoln

Purple Horse Mint near Palmyra

THE PRAIRIES

Purple Horse Mint, shown near Palmyra, is a native flower familiar to Natives and pioneers. Left: Nine Mile Prairie exists within sight of the state capitol. Page 36-37: Hitchcock County is shortgrass country. Of a nearby station of the Leavenworth and Pike's Peak Express stage line, newspaperman Horace Greeley wrote in 1859, "I would match this station and its surroundings against any other scene on our continent for desolation."

Shortgrass prairie, Hitchcock County

The Sandhills, North of Arthur

THE SANDHILLS

Before the Sandhills region was cattle country, it was home to bison, which can still be seen on numerous ranches and at Fort Niobrara National Wildlife Refuge near Valentine. Page 38-39: The Sandhills cover one-fourth of the state. The hills themselves are stabilized sand dunes. The sandy soil soaks up rain, forming a vast aquifer.

Fort Niobrara National Wildlife Refuge, Cherry County

North Platte River, Morrill County

Lover's Leap, Dawes County

Near Harrison, Sioux County

THE WEST

Cowboy culture is strong in the state's northwest corner. Left: Lover's Leap is one of the distinctive buttes of the Pine Ridge. Page 42-43: The marked grave of Oregon Trail pioneer Amanda Lamme stands near this spot along the North Platte River. Lamme died of cholera here in 1850. Page 46-47: Camp Sheridan and Spotted Tail Agency were near these buttes. Crazy Horse surrendered at the agency in 1877. He was murdered at Fort Robinson the next day. Some say he was buried here.

Camp Sheridan and Spotted Tail Agency, Sheridan County

Fort Atkinson, Washington County

Winnebago Tribe, Thurston County

EXPLORERS AND SOLDIERS

Before Nebraska was settled, it was visited by explorers and traders, and crossed by half a million pioneers bound for points farther west. For Nebraska's Native population, the days of independence were coming to an end.

IN 1541, FRANCISCO VASQUEZ CORONADO searched for cities of gold on the Great Plains of North America. He'd been told that in the Kingdom of Quivira, even the poor ate from gold dishes.

Coronado was apparently the first European to be hoodwinked by tales of easy wealth on the Plains. He would not be the last. His infamous wild goose chase was long reckoned to be the opening chapter of Nebraska exploration.

But it really doesn't matter that Coronado likely got no farther north than central Kansas. The notion that the first white men to set foot in Nebraska were drawn by outrageous

lies about cities of gold is just too good of a story to let go. It's a true story about the Great Plains, and that's close enough.

And the truth is that for many years, Nebraska's visitors were Spanish or French soldiers and traders who also harbored ideas of easy wealth, but who never figured out how to make this strange land pay. The best they could do was to scheme and build shaky alliances with Native peoples in hopes of keeping their European rivals out.

In 1803, the complex rivalries of European politics resulted in the United States getting the opportunity to buy Louisiana – which at the time was reckoned as the entire region between

Above: Dating to 1866, the Winnebago tribe's annual powwow is America's longest-running powwow open to the public. Left: In 1820, Fort Atkinson became the U.S. Army's westernmost outpost. A thousand people lived here, many weeks travel from St. Louis, the nearest city. The fort was built to protect the Missouri River fur trade. In 1823, soldiers traveled upstream to attack the Arikara Indians in reprisal for an attack on a fur trading party.

the Mississippi River and the Rocky Mountains. The following year, a group of American explorers ventured from St. Louis up the Missouri River. They were sent to report on this new Louisiana country, and if possible to find a water route connecting it to the Pacific.

LEWIS AND CLARK

The storm whipped the Missouri River into whitecaps that pounded the keelboat's starboard bow. The waves "would have thrown her up on the sand island, dashed to pieces in an instant," William Clark wrote later that day, "had not the party leaped out on the leeward side and kept her off with the assistance of the anchor and cable, until the *storm* was over."

It was July 14, 1804, and Clark was writing from camp near present-day Indian Cave State Park in southeast Nebraska. A few days earlier, the Corps of Discovery had entered that portion of the Missouri River that borders Nebraska. From here up to Lynch, the Nebraska border is now dotted with markers showing their campsites.

The markers can't convey how difficult it was for 30-some men to move a 30-ton keelboat and two smaller boats day after day against the current. They rowed in deep water, poled in shallow water. Some days they raised the sail. Other days the only way to make headway was to haul the boat by rope from shore. They entered present-day Nebraska on July 11 and left it on September 8.

It was a busy two months. Near present-day Fort Atkinson, Lewis and Clark held their first council with Native Americans to convince an Otoe and Missouri delegation that the Great White Father really had the Indians' best interests at heart.

The company's first deserter, Pvt. Moses Reed, received about 500 lashes while running a gauntlet through the company near Sioux City, Iowa. Sgt. Charles Floyd died of natural causes, Capt. Lewis accidentally poisoned himself with mineral samples near Ponca State Park, and Pvt. George Shannon got lost and went hungry for two weeks.

Out in the wilderness, the margin between life and death was a thin one. And if some of the men didn't understand that when they set out, the events of August certainly made it clear. Their long adventure was only beginning.

THE FUR TRADE

In the early 20th century, a young poet living in Bancroft, Neb., decided that the story of the West from the fur trade through the end of the Indian Wars was as worthy of epic treatment as anything from the world of Homer or Virgil.

Fur traders and trappers were usually considered too rough and uncouth to be fitting subjects of literature. But John G. Neihardt, who became Nebraska's Poet Laureate, spent 29

years writing *A Cycle of the West*. Three of the cycle's five book-length poems are about "mountain men" of the fur trade era. Of one important Missouri River expedition he wrote,

"One hundred strong they flocked to Ashley's call
That spring of eighteen hundred twenty-two;
For tales of wealth, out-legending Peru,
Came wind-blown from Missouri's distant springs,
And that old sireny of unknown things
Bewitched them…"

They were men like Coronado, in other words.

The Western trade began because fur was valuable – particularly beaver, which was used to the make expensive top hats for gentlemen. Companies sent trappers out into the wilderness, and opened isolated posts for trade with Indians. In 1820, the government built Fort Atkinson at Lewis and Clark's "Council Bluff" to protect the growing Missouri River trade. At the time it was the Army's westernmost outpost.

Trading posts existed in various locations. In Nebraska, for example, the city of Bellevue began as a trading post, and the site of James Bordeaux's 1846 post near Chadron is preserved today as the Museum of the Fur Trade. These and others were important points of contact between Americans and Native Americans in the pre-settlement era.

The trappers, meanwhile, roamed the wilderness in search of beaver. Regarding exploration, government-backed expeditions like that of Lewis and Clark were the exception – most of the West was discovered by mountain men. Among other things, their knowledge led to the establishment of the Oregon Trail.

Epic stuff, indeed.

PIONEER TRAILS

From the 1840s to the 1860s, some half million emigrants passed through Nebraska on their way west. They sought farms in Oregon, gold in California, or a Mormon promised land along the shores of the Great Salt Lake.

The main trail started at Independence, Mo., and came up through southeast Nebraska, then followed the Platte River west. Near Ash Hollow, it descended into the North Platte valley down a steep hill wryly dubbed Windlass Hill. The saying, not meant literally, was that you had to let your wagon down the slope with a windlass. Then it was on past Courthouse and Jail Rocks, Chimney Rock and Scotts Bluff.

Fifteen miles a day was a good average over the Plains. The idea was to leave the Missouri River by April 15 and make it to South Pass (in central Wyoming) by the Fourth of July. Winter was always on a traveler's mind.

Emigrants and their livestock tended to befoul the creeks and rivers from which they drank. Partly as a result, many

Lewis and Clark first encountered prairie dogs in Boyd County. After much futile digging, they "caught one alive by pouring a great quantity of water in his hole."

Lewis and Clark Discover Prairie Dogs, Boyd County

people died from cholera and other germ-borne illnesses.

Accidental deaths were common, too. Despite the popular image of circled wagons and whooping Indians on horseback, pioneers were more likely to shoot themselves by accident than to get shot on purpose by an Indian.

In all, odds of death along the trail were about one in 17. Historians debate whether the risk exceeded that of staying home in the hazardous, disease-ridden good old days.

None of this diminishes the accomplishment of those who completed the long journey in one piece. Sometimes we assume that pioneers were tougher and smarter than we are today. In fact, most emigrants were ordinary people who didn't know what they were getting themselves into. They made life-changing decisions based on questionable information. They complained, laughed, bickered, sang songs and told stories. Sometimes they got away with terrible mistakes. Sometimes they paid with their lives. Many turned back, many died along the way (sometimes for no apparent reason), but most people figured they could make it if they only stuck together and kept moving.

The story of the Oregon Trail, in other words, is the story of the human race in miniature.

Soldiers and Indians

Along Highway 26 west of Lewellen stands a marker labeled "The Battle of Blue Water." With a name like that, you just know it's going to be an exciting story. The battlefield itself is on private property, but you can get a pretty good idea just by driving to where Blue Creek emerges from its broad canyon near Lewellen. You can imagine Gen. Harney and his blue-coated men camping at nearby Ash Hollow.

And then you find out what really happened here in 1855 – how Harney attacked an unsuspecting Lakota camp, killing as many as half of the 250 people present, and how the soldiers fired into caves where women and children were cowering, how afterward the tipis and meat and possessions were burned in great bonfires so that survivors would starve during the coming winter.

That's what it's like to read the history of the Indian Wars. There are exciting tales involving soldiers, horses and frontier forts. But the stories are dark, and they rarely have happy endings. Blue Water was neither a mistake nor an anomaly. Harney's strategy became a model for later massacres by commanders such as Chivington and Custer.

Above: Lewis and Clark called it "The Tower"; today the Boyd County butte is known as Old Baldy.
They spent a day here catching a prairie dog to send home to President Thomas Jefferson.

Old Baldy, or "The Tower," Boyd County

The nature of warfare is that it either results from, or ends in, seeing one's adversaries as less than fully human. That is true regardless of race or culture: In 1873, at a place in southwestern Nebraska since known as Massacre Canyon, a band of Lakota warriors launched a surprise attack against a Pawnee hunting camp. They left the field littered with the bodies of about 70 men, women and children.

Even Lewis and Clark were too late to see Plains tribes at their peak. Smallpox had already begun to devastate the tribes they met along the way. Disease, alcohol, increased warfare, the fur trade and the resulting decline of wild game, all reduced Native Nebraskans to a sorry state before whites began entering the territory in large numbers. Likewise, soldiers at Nebraska's forts usually saw Native peoples in decline.

The conquest of the Great Plains was done mostly without open warfare. It was more of a gradual hemming in, accomplished by a series of treaties negotiated under threat of force and, without exception, subsequently broken by the government which had imposed them.

As a result, the American conscience has never been fully at rest with this part of our heritage. But it's a good sign that it bothers us. Like a person of ideals, a nation of ideals *should* suffer a guilty conscience from time to time, allowing conscience to teach better behavior.

With that in mind, our choice of heroes is telling. In the 1860s, Red Cloud led the most successful war ever fought against the United States by an Indian nation; in 2000, the Lakota chief was voted into the Nebraska Hall of Fame. Crazy Horse, murdered at Fort Robinson in 1877, is today revered by the descendants of people who once feared and hated him. His story is told in a sympathetic 1942 biography that remains one of the best-loved books by one of Nebraska's best-loved authors, Mari Sandoz.

And then there is Standing Bear, a Ponca chief and Nebraska Hall of Fame inductee. After his people were forcibly removed from their northeast Nebraska homeland, he fought the United States in court – the first Native American to do so. He didn't get his land back, but won an important victory in an 1879 Omaha trial: For the first time, a federal court ruled that an Indian was a person under the law. Today a Missouri River bridge near Standing Bear's old home bears his name, and inside the state capitol, the chief is immortalized in a mural titled, appropriately, "The Ideal of Freedom."

Page 54-55: It is easy to imagine yourself a part of the Corps of Discovery's adventure when you're standing on a replica of the 30-ton keelboat at the Lewis and Clark Center in Nebraska City.

Missouri River Basin Lewis and Clark Interpretive Trail and Visitor Center, Nebraska City

John G. Neihardt Center, Bancroft

THE FUR TRADE

Nebraska Poet Laureate John G. Neihardt wrote of the Plains Indians and Western history from the fur trade era through the end of the Indian Wars. The Neihardt Center in Bancroft, where the poet used to live, is designed according to the vision of Lakota holy man Black Elk. Right, a historical re-enactor brings the fur trade era to life near Chadron, home of the Museum of the Fur Trade at the site of James Bordeaux's trading post.

Fur traders explore Nebraska, Dawes County

Mormon Trail, Buffalo County

On the Trail

Thousands of Mormons, too poor to afford horses or oxen, hauled their possessions to Utah in handcarts. Page 60-61: The most written-about landmark on the entire trail was Chimney Rock. The tip of the spire is 325 feet above the base. It was visible to travelers for three or four days as they passed by.

Chimney Rock, Morrill County

Battle of Blue Water, Garden County

BLUE CREEK

Near Lewellen, Blue Creek
flows into the North Platte
River. In 1855, soldiers
attacked a Lakota hunting
camp near here, an event
known as the Battle of Blue
Water or the Harney Mas-
sacre. The soldiers camped
nearby at Ash Hollow,
where a spring-fed pond
was an important stopping
place for travelers on the
Oregon and Mormon trails.

NATIVE NEBRASKA

Historic Plains Indians are pictured at Fort Robinson, which started as a frontier outpost during the Sioux Wars. Right, a child at the Northern Ponca Powwow in Niobrara. Though the Ponca were forcibly removed from their Nebraska lands in the 1870s, a portion of the tribe returned with Chief Standing Bear. Their descendants remain to this day.

Northern Ponca Powwow, Niobrara

Standing Bear Bridge, Knox County

Chief Standing Bear Day at State Capitol

NATIVE HERO

Chief Standing Bear Day at the
State Capitol, May 12, 2007. Left,
at Niobrara, Neb., the Standing
Bear Bridge spans the Missouri
River in the part of Nebraska to
which Standing Bear's people
wanted so badly to return.

Fort Atkinson, Washington County

Gatling gun, Dodge County

ARMY LIFE

A Gatling gun, an early machine gun invented at the time of the Civil War, is demonstrated in Fremont. Page 68-69: Re-enactors portray 1820s Army life at Fort Atkinson. Page 72-73: Built to protect settlers and Pawnees from raiding Lakotas, Fort Hartsuff was used 1874-1881.

Fort Hartsuff State Historical Park, Valley County

Kimball County

Homestead National Monument, Beatrice

SETTLEMENT

For the pioneers, Nebraska was a new land unlike any place they'd lived before. As towns and farms and ranches sprouted on the prairies, it remained to be seen which of the newcomers would last.

OSES SYDENHAM was a pioneer, which is to say, an optimist. A pioneer could see a well-tended farm where others saw only virgin prairie, or imagine a great city where others saw only a rude cluster of soddies and tarpaper shacks. Pioneer vision favored possibility over reality. By that measure, today's town boosters have nothing on their pioneer forebears.

And most pioneers had nothing on Moses Sydenham. In 1872, he platted a town west of the recently-abandoned Fort Kearny. Never mind that the fort's adjacent "Dobytown" settlement had long been notorious as the place, in the words of one Army officer, "where the toughs of the country met and had their frolics. Large quantities of the meanest whisky on earth were consumed here…."

Sydenham called his new town Centoria, promoted it as the center of the nation, and tried first to make it the capital of Nebraska, and then of the United States. In his newspaper, the *Central Star*, he argued persistently that the federal government already owned all the land it needed at the site of the abandoned fort. Like so many big dreams, Centoria soon faded. It was done in by an upstart called Kearney Junction.

But Sydenham's vision differed from that of his neighbors only in scale. Pioneers didn't come to the Nebraska frontier because they wanted to live in isolated dugouts. They came because they wanted to prosper on farms and in cities, and they saw this as their best (and perhaps only) chance to do that.

Everything would have to be built from scratch. But looking out on the endless land, a pioneer could see it all clearly, as if it was there already.

HUMBLE ORIGINS

At Morgan Park in Callaway stands Custer County's original courthouse. It doesn't have a Romanesque stone inscription ("CVSTER COVNTY COVRT HOVSE") above neo-classical pillars like the 1912 building in Broken Bow. The first courthouse is a log cabin.

Above: Homestead National Monument, Beatrice.
Left: Kimball County

Built in 1876 on a local ranch, it was designated a courthouse a year later when the county was organized. It served for seven years, then became a private residence. Finally it was abandoned and was eventually moved into town as a memorial to the county's pioneer days.

Not every county still has its old courthouse, and not every town still has its old schools or churches. And even when they do, what they have probably isn't the original. The limestone courthouses with their solemn pillars, or the white country churches with their bells and tall steeples, are almost certainly not the first buildings to house their respective institutions.

In each case, the original was probably a log cabin, sod house or dugout. That was the way of the frontier. People wanted the trappings of civilization as quickly as possible, even if they had to make do regarding building materials. The result was sometimes a succession of buildings, each outdoing the last for size and grandeur.

Omaha's Capitol Hill is one of the best examples. For more than a century, the stately Central High School has occupied the hilltop. Some Omahans, dimly aware of the hill's history, say the building used to be the courthouse. It wasn't – though to look at it you could be forgiven for thinking so. It is actually the third building to occupy that hill. A smaller, Victorian high school preceded the current building, and the old territorial capitol preceded that.

Pioneers weren't concerned with preserving their town's early structures. If anything, they were eager to erase the physical evidence of their humble origins, because the humility of pioneer life was a touchy subject. In letters and diaries, settlers sometimes complained about their circumstances – but let a loved one from back East suggest that Nebraska was less than civilized, and the settler in her cabin might become defensive:

"Now perhaps Camille and the other girls will think, well I don't see how Phebe can be willing to live in such a heathenish country," wrote Phebe Clark of Fort Calhoun in 1856. "WHY! My Goodness Gracious! Girls, we are not at all out of the world. People think, act, talk, walk and halloo 'Hurrah for Buchanan' [elected to the Presidency that year] just as they do in the states exactly… We have two horses and a buggy, a lumber wagon and yoke of cattle, a cow and calf, a pig, sixteen chickens, a cat and dog, and a BABY."

ETHNIC SETTLEMENTS

"If I told my schoolmates that Lena Lingard's grandfather was a clergyman, and much respected in Norway, they looked at me blankly. What did it matter? All foreigners were ignorant people who couldn't speak English."

– Willa Cather, *My Ántonia*

One of the surprising things about pioneer-era Nebraska is how foreign it was. By 1880, more than half of Nebraskans were either foreign-born or had at least one foreign-born parent. Among many other groups, there were Swedes in Stromsburg, Danes in Dannebrog, Irish in O'Neill, Czechs in Wilber, and Germans… well, everywhere you looked. During an 1889 tour of America, Rudyard Kipling perceived Omaha to be "populated entirely by Germans, Poles, Slavs, Hungarians, Croats, Magyars, and all the scum of the Eastern European States…."

A lot of Americans thought it was perfectly acceptable to talk about somebody else's ethnicity like that. One of the curious things about this nation of immigrants is how few generations it takes before newcomers turn their condescension upon people who got off the boat after they did. At the same time, no other nation has so successfully absorbed so many people of diverse nationalities.

Most Nebraska communities were built by mixed ethnic populations, but a fair number of towns were founded by settlers from a single country. Coming to America was a scary thing. It was comforting to surround oneself with people who shared your language and traditions.

And while all communities became Americanized, cultural heritage persisted longer where people shared an ethnic identity. German was still spoken in many homes and churches when it became vilified during the anti-German hysteria of World War I. For several years after the war it was illegal in Nebraska to teach any modern foreign language in private or parochial elementary schools. German-American Lutherans, who wanted their kids to be able to participate in German-language church services, challenged the law all the way to the U.S. Supreme Court – and won.

Other foreign languages also persisted. West of Shickley in southeast Nebraska, for example, Stockholm Lutheran Church held services in Swedish as late as 1937. And older residents in Crete remember when Czech was heard as frequently on downtown streets as Spanish is today.

No historical markers yet commemorate Nebraska's Latin American immigrants, who were first recruited to work in western Nebraska's sugar beet fields in the 1920s. Today, Scottsbluff and Gering are about 25 percent Latino, and multi-generation Mexican-American families are common there. Elsewhere in the state – in cities like Lexington, Grand Island, Omaha and South Sioux City – Latino immigration is more recent. Partly because of an ongoing debate about illegal immigration, and partly because of the old suspicion of outsiders, the latest newcomers are often talked as if they are ignorant Norwegians from Willa Cather's day.

More than any other group, African-Americans have been forced to stick together. A few Nebraska settlements were founded by black settlers (none remain today), and the all-black 9th and 10th U.S. Cavalry regiments (whom the Indians

Custer County's first courthouse stands in a city park in Callaway. Page 78-79: A modern cowboy isn't going as far as riders in the Chadron-Chicago Cowboy Race of 1893.

Custer County's First Courthouse, Callaway

called "Buffalo Soldiers") were stationed at Fort Robinson from the 1880s through the 1900s. But then as now, most black Nebraskans lived in Omaha, where systematic housing discrimination (to say nothing of all the other manifestations of prejudice) restricted black residents to homes on the Near North Side. Nebraska did not ban housing discrimination until 1969.

Too often, the story of race and ethnicity has been about one group assuming the inferiority of another group. The ethnic celebrations that have grown up around the state show a better way – teaching us to appreciate how each group is a distinctive and valuable part of a larger whole.

FARMING

First you had to break the sod. Prairie grass stretched from horizon to horizon, and pioneers soon learned one of its secrets: Most of the plant lies underground in a dense, tough network of roots.

At one time, the breaking of native prairie was done with a huge cast-iron plow pulled by as many as seven yokes of oxen. By the time Nebraska was settled, however, John Deere's famous polished steel plow had made it possible for a farmer with a single yoke of oxen or a three-horse hitch to cut a clean furrow through virgin prairie. Some farmers said the snapping roots sounded like pistol fire. Others compared the sound of "sod busting" to that of ripping fabric.

Plowing was also a good way to build a home. In the 1880s, a new plow was designed to cut strips of sod a foot wide and four inches thick – just the right size to use as bricks for your sod house. Just half an acre of prairie sod was enough to build a snug, 320-square-foot home.

Sod busting had another big advantage, or so people thought: It changed the climate. Thanks to the coincidence of a period of extensive sod-breaking with a good stretch of wet years, people hypothesized that plowed fields absorbed more moisture, which then evaporated and came back as increased rainfall. The idea was summed up in the expression "rain follows the plow." It was the greatest notion to hit the Plains since Coronado's cities of gold – and by the 1890s proved to be equally delusional.

Chadron-Chicago Cowboy Race

Living on a Nebraska farm often meant coping with scarce wood and water. It meant surviving blizzards, hailstorms, tornadoes, prairie fires, grasshoppers and years of drought. It meant railroad monopolies and high shipping rates. It meant mortgages, low crop prices and living day to day, year to year on the edge of losing all you'd worked for.

Today the farmland remains, though most of the old farmsteads are gone. Across the state, annual horse-plowing events show how generations of farmers used to work the land. In Neligh, Champion and Omaha, historic mills still stand, remnants of the days when a town had a big advantage over its neighbors if it had a local mill to process grain before it was shipped.

On the small farms, only the smart, strong and stubborn remained long on the land – and sometimes even these qualities weren't enough. But there was something about the notion of living on your own farm, out in the wide-open country and not packed cheek-by-jowl in a city, doing your own work, being your own boss, and building something you could hand down to the next generation. Taken together, it was a powerful idea. And still is.

THE COWBOY WAY

Andy Adams was all set to enjoy Ogallala. He was part of cattle drive coming up from Texas in the summer of 1882, and got paid upon arrival at the "Gomorrah of the cattle trail."

"From amongst its half hundred buildings," Adams wrote in his 1903 memoir, *Log of a Cowboy*, "no church spire pointed upward, but instead three fourths of its business houses were dance halls, gambling houses, and saloons. We all knew the town by reputation… for the ends of the earth's iniquity had gathered in Ogallala."

To hear Adams tell it, Ogallala was cowboy heaven – drinking and gambling, a horse race in the street, drawn pistols at a card game, even a fiddling contest that was interrupted by the sound of gunfire from a nearby restaurant. The ladies at the Dew-Drop-Inn dance hall "all were there in tinsel and paint, practicing a careless exposure of their charms."

During the 1870s and '80s, cowboys drove herds of longhorn cattle from Texas to Nebraska so the beef could be shipped east on the Union Pacific Railroad. Much of the lore of the Wild West comes from the brief cattle trail era. And

A.B., Zack and Don Cox, Cherry County

maybe everything got bigger in Andy Adams' memory as the years passed, but he wasn't the only one to describe Ogallala that way.

In time, settlement on the Great Plains put an end to the "long drives." But by then Nebraska didn't need Texas cattle. It was proving to be excellent cattle country in its own right.

Nebraska's early cattlemen worked on the open range. They'd homestead or buy enough land to ensure access to water, then graze their herds on the enormous expanse of public land, paying neither rent nor taxes. For a while, it was highly profitable – a new version of Coronado's old dream of easy wealth on the Plains.

Then the terrible blizzards of 1885-86 and 1886-87 reminded cattlemen that nothing is easy for long on the Plains. Entire herds – representing vast fortunes – lay frozen to death on the fields.

Settlers posed another challenge. They claimed homesteads on public land that the cattlemen were using as their own. Sometimes the cattlemen cut the settlers' newfangled barbed-wire fences. Sometimes they resorted to intimidation and murder.

For the past century, the old cowboy towns and surrounding rangeland have been pretty quiet. Even Ogallala has grown respectable, though it enjoys reliving its rowdy past with summer shows and mock gunfights on Front Street. Elsewhere, cowboy action shooting groups practice riding and shooting – in tribute both to the old days and to the tales and movies that mythologized them.

But the Nebraska cowboy isn't only a myth or a memory. Brandings are still an annual working event, and ranch hands still test their skills and courage at small town rodeos. Along roads across the state, you may still have to stop now and then while men (and women) on horseback drive a herd of cattle across the road. Truth is, those young men following the Western Trail up from Texas may have been colorful, but they were amateurs compared to today's ranch families, many of whom have been working the land for four or five generations.

Near Stockville, Frontier County

RANCH LIFE   While a cattle branding was underway back at the ranch, these Frontier County girls are on their way to Grandma's house to help prepare lunch for the hands. Left, Don Cox's great-grandfather, Eck Cox, was a Kinkaider. He settled in the Sandhills in 1907, three years after the Kinkaid Act permitted each homesteader to claim a square mile of land in parts of Nebraska.

Horse-drawn hay cutting, Saunders County

HORSES AND TRACTOR

Farmers demonstrate old-time haying skills on a farm in Saunders County. Right: Near the site of Camp Sheridan and Spotted Tail Agency in the Panhandle, hay is cut using equipment that's a little more modern.

Camp Sheridan and Spotted Tail Agency, Sheridan County

Brewster ranch, Blaine County

Jansen wheat harvest, Jefferson County

West Point hog farm, Cuming County

On the Farm

One could appropriately place historic markers at thousands of Nebraska farms where traditions of the family farm remain amid modern agriculture. Left to right: Showing off fresh-laid multi-colored eggs near the Sandhills town of Brewster. Wheat harvest in the southeastern town of Jansen. And near West Point, the Guenthers live on a farm that's been in their family more than a century. In addition to working on the farm, Dad works full-time at a local feedlot.

Norwegian Lutheran Church, Furnas County

Friedensau Church, Thayer County

Swedish Crosses Cemetery, Dawson County

ETHNIC NEBRASKA

North of Gothenburg, three children are buried under traditional Swedish crosses made in the 1880s by their grandfather, who was the town's first blacksmith. Left: The German Lutheran community of Friedensau was founded in 1874 and abandoned 13 years later when the railroad came to nearby Deshler instead. Buildings were moved; only Trinity Lutheran Church remains. Page 86-87: The 1904 Norwegian Lutheran Church near Holbrook.

Czech Festival in July, Dwight.

El Vaquero pottery store, South Omaha Neighborhood

MANY CULTURES   El Vaquero Imports is
part of the thriving "South O" business district in Omaha.
Left: The town of Dwight celebrates an annual Czech Festival in July.

State Capitol, Lincoln

Peterson-Yanney Memorial Bell Tower at University of Nebraska-Kearney

DEVELOPMENT

The frontier closed (or did it?) and Nebraska entered the 20th century. More people meant more changes, more big dreams, and more stories.

AT WHAT POINT does a frontier cease to be a frontier? In 1893, historian Frederick Jackson Turner delivered a famous lecture in which he noted that "the frontier has gone, and with its going has closed the first period of American history."

But when did the frontier really close in Nebraska? Turner said that the "most significant thing about the American frontier is that it lies at the hither edge of free land." By that measure, much of Nebraska remained a frontier at least into the 1920s. Turner also noted that the Census Bureau defined frontier as the boundary of settlement with a population density of two people per square mile. By that measure, 16 Nebraska counties qualified as frontier in 2000.

Nevertheless, a visible transition took place from the earliest days of settlement. Nebraska towns were pretty much all founded within a 50-year period, and like a slow-moving wave across the state from east to west, towns were built, rebuilt, and rebuilt again, farms were plowed and fenced, expanded and improved... and gradually the state was covered with larger farms, bigger and more substantial buildings, dams and irrigation projects, highways and bridges, factories and military bases. The process has been going on long enough that many of these formerly shining examples of Progress have grown quaint – and many bear historical markers telling their story.

At what point did Nebraska's pioneer period end? To hear folklorist and author Roger Welsch tell it, it hasn't. Even the frequency of record-setting weather reminds us that we haven't been here long enough to really understand the place. People of the future, he believes, will count us among Nebraska's pioneering generations.

Above: Peterson-Yanney Memorial Bell Tower at the University of Nebraska-Kearney.
Left: Built 1922-1932, the Nebraska State Capitol is the fifth building to house Nebraska's legislature.

Nebraska Statehood Memorial, near Kennard House and State Capitol

BUILDING BIGGER AND BETTER

Tales of theft and robbery aren't difficult to find across Nebraska, whether it's Sam Bass and the Big Springs train robbery of 1877, or stories about Nebraska horse thief extraordinaire Doc Middleton. But in many counties, the best story of historic thievery involves ordinary citizens and a county seat.

Take Wahoo, for example. An 1873 county election moved the seat of Saunders County there from Ashland. Folks in Ashland complained that Wahoo cast more votes than it had people. In Wahoo, the story is still told (with some pride) that after the election, Wahoo men bribed an Ashland man to leave the courthouse doors unlocked. County records were then quietly hustled away to Wahoo before Ashland knew what was happening.

Maybe the contested nature of county seats was part of the motivation behind the building of grand courthouses. One advantage of a massive, brick edifice that's often overlooked today is that it's hard to move. Maybe a gang of Wahooligans will break in and steal the county records, but at least they can't pick up the courthouse itself and cart it away... as Alliance did to Hemingford in 1899, when after an election the two-story wooden Box Butte County Courthouse was loaded onto a train and hauled 18 precarious miles to Alliance.

Being the county seat was like being located along a railroad: It could determine whether a town survived or not. Most towns did not. The future of Nebraska small towns was, and remains, precarious. For the people's sake, it was important to build in a way that spoke of permanence and stability.

Not that people in the old days always took more pride or showed more skill in construction than we do today. We see only their masterpieces, not their mistakes. Even when building their most important institutions, our ancestors erected their share of junk.

The State Capitol in Lincoln, for example, is arguably the finest and most original of the 50 state capitols – but it is also Nebraska's first decent capitol *in five tries*. The first territorial capitol in Omaha was a small brick building that quickly proved inadequate. The second, atop Capitol Hill, started falling apart before it was finished. The third (the first state capitol in Lincoln) soon began to crumble. The fourth began to settle structurally after only a few decades. But the fifth capitol, built 1922-1932, is one for the ages.

We'll just say the others were for practice.

TRANSFORMING OUR WATERWAYS

As Nebraska's population grew, so did the people's ability to alter nature. The most obvious example is the transformation of the prairie into cropland and pasture. But the transformation of the state's waterways is also a story of great consequence.

Compared to the great dams and reservoirs of the 20th century, the early projects were small in scale, yet ambitious. The Kearney Canal was completed in 1886, and a few years later began providing hydroelectric power to the rapidly

Above: Lincoln, then known as Lancaster, was a village of about 50 residents when it was selected as the state capital in 1867, the year of Nebraska statehood.

State Capitol, Memorial Chamber on 14th floor

growing town. For 75 cents a month per lamp, Kearney residents could enjoy incandescent electric lighting. Electric trolleys (the first in the state) carried passengers across town, and the canal even powered turbines at a cotton mill – just about the last type of factory you'd expect to find in Nebraska. The cotton was brought in by train from the South.

Kearney's boom years ended painfully during the drought and economic depression of the 1890s, but Nebraska's water-powered dreams wouldn't die. The 20th century would see the construction of dozens of reservoirs – most notably, Lake C.W. McConaughy, Nebraska's largest above-ground body of water.

So effective has Nebraska been in diverting its surface water and groundwater for agriculture that it is reaching the limits of what is available. River ecosystems are threatened, and Nebraska's ancient underground sea – the Ogallala Aquifer – is being depleted in some areas. If the challenge of the 20th century was learning how to harness water, the challenge of the 21st will be learning to live within nature's limits.

All this would have been inconceivable to earlier generations of Nebraskans, who saw such vast resources that they thought them inexhaustible.

HIGHER EDUCATION

An institution of higher learning with the name "Mallalieu University" sounds believable as long as one assumes that it's located somewhere in France and dates back centuries.

Place it in Bartley, Neb., population 350, and it sounds a little farfetched. Open it in 1886, the same year the town was founded, and it sounds like a pipe-dream.

And maybe it was. But it was a good dream while it lasted.

You don't have to read very far into the history of prairie pioneers before you uncover a strong current of anti-intellectualism. Most settlers could read and write, but many saw no use in book learning that went beyond that. They respected practical knowledge that addressed problems of survival. The harsh and unfamiliar Plains environment enforced that kind of intellectual discipline. Literature and philosophy would neither harvest your crops nor heal your sick cow.

But that's only one side of the story. The countryside was dotted with small towns, every one of which believed it was on its way to becoming an important city. Often, one or more residents of a future city or owners of future prosperous farms saw the need not only for a schoolhouse and the three R's, but for a local university.

Residents of Peru, for example, organized and financed a college they called Mount Vernon Seminary and offered it to the Methodist Conference. When the Methodists turned them down, residents offered the school to the state. It became Nebraska State Normal School and held its first classes in 1867, just months after Nebraska became a state. Thus, Nebraska's first state-supported college was not the University of Nebraska (founded two years later), but the school now known as Peru State College. And it came about not because of the state, but because of ambitious townspeople who took

Above: Omaha artist Stephen Cornelius Roberts spent seven years painting eight murals for the Capitol's Memorial Chamber. The 7-by-12-foot murals depict heroic enterprises of Nebraska.

the future of education into their own hands. Other colleges across Nebraska have similar stories.

Such as Bartley's Mallalieu University. Like the town itself, the university was founded by Rev. Allen Bartley and named for a Methodist bishop.

Bartley's town survived, but his school did not. Though Mallalieu held classes for a few years, even graduating some students, its first permanent building was never completed. After financial troubles closed the school, the bricks were used to build Bartley Methodist Church, which is all that remains of this particular pioneer dream of higher education.

THE AUTOMOBILE ERA

The future rolled into Omaha on July 12, 1903, riding on pneumatic tires and powered by a two-cylinder, 20-horsepower engine. It wasn't the first automobile the city had seen, but it was the first to arrive after crossing half a continent.

Already in Kearney, Grand Island, Columbus and other towns, telegraph reports had preceded the auto's arrival, and spectators gathered to see Dr. Horatio Nelson Jackson, "The Mad Doctor," who was attempting to drive from San Francisco to New York City.

The retired 31-year-old physician could afford harebrained quests. He had married a wealthy heiress, whose money supported his passions for travel, racehorses, and what he called the "newfangled horseless buggy." To win a $50 bet, Nelson became the first man to cross the continent (and Nebraska) by automobile. It took him 63 days and cost $8,000.

As automobiles became more affordable, people began to travel for pleasure in a way they had not done before, visiting distant locations without confinement to railroad tracks or schedules. They drove through the main street of every town (for there were no bypasses), ate at local diners (no chain restaurants), met other travelers at roadside campgrounds, got lost, got stuck – and in the process, got a clearer sense of the country and people beyond their hometowns. That, many people believed, would further unify the nation.

And when a cross-country "highway" was mapped out in 1913, connecting countless farm roads and dirt paths, it was named, patriotically, in honor of Abraham Lincoln. It was to be a highway of the people, by the people, for the people.

Travelers wanted improved roads, but Nebraska was slow to develop its highway system. In the 1920s, many rural residents (about half the state's population at the time) opposed spending money on anything but farm-to-market roads. One state representative argued that highways promoted joyriding.

Maybe so, but eventually Nebraskans decided that that might not be such a bad thing.

NEBRASKA AT WAR

East of Alliance, Highway 2 passes through the lake country of the Sandhills, arguably the most beautiful part of the vast Sandhills region. Near the barely-inhabited town of Antioch, for no apparent reason you come upon concrete arches and crumbling walls standing incongruously in a pasture. Beside the highway, a historical marker tells the story. The Sandhills are sometimes described as isolated, but these ruins are the result of cotton-belt agriculture and of a war that was fought half a world away.

When World War I began in 1914, the United States was soon cut off from European sources of potash, a chemical compound that was used in fertilizer for cotton fields. When chemists discovered that this valuable material could be made from the alkaline lakes of the Sandhills, a new industry was born. Antioch became a boomtown.

Then the war ended, cheaper imports resumed, and the Sandhills potash industry ended. Antioch's rise and fall happened in the space of five years.

Though they aren't directly related to the U.S. war effort, the ruins are an early example of how foreign wars would alter the Nebraska landscape in the 20th century. World War II would leave a bigger mark.

Across Nebraska, the land still bears traces of what many Americans still refer to simply as "The War." Nebraska's geography – safely distant from the coasts, with relatively level terrain and a sparse population – made it desirable to military planners. During the war, Nebraska was home to a dozen different Army airfields, numerous prisoner of war facilities, and various wartime industries.

Paratroopers practiced for D-Day in Alliance; bombers flew mock nighttime raids over a blacked-out McCook; war dogs trained at Fort Robinson; the nation's largest inland naval ammunition depot was built in Hastings; a factory turned out thousands of bombers in Bellevue, including the atomic-bomb-carrying *Enola Gay;* a hundred thousand German prisoners passed through Camp Atlanta near Holdrege, most bound for smaller camps around the state; volunteers in North Platte met every single troop train with free food and gifts, using their ration stamps to serve six million soldiers over the course of the war. This is only a partial list.

Today, some of Nebraska's wartime facilities have vanished, but others remain – if you know where to look. Travelers still wonder about the strange earthen "igloos" that line Highway 6 near Hastings, or the sprawling, abandoned cities near Sidney and Grand Island – sites that were dedicated to the manufacture or storage of ammunition. These and others are evidence of Nebraska's good geographic fortune – not merely that it was chosen for such facilities, but that it was chosen precisely because it was about as far from the war's bloodshed and destruction as one could get. 🦅

Built between 1900 and 1912, Omaha's Central High School is built atop Capitol Hill, where the Nebraska Territorial Capitol once stood.

Central High School, Omaha

COUNTY COURTHOUSE

In many counties, the courthouse was the grandest building, a point of civil pride in the county seat. In Minden's town square, the Classical Revival-style Kearney County Courthouse was built in 1907.

Kearney County Courthouse, Minden

Fillmore County Courthouse, Geneva

Thayer County Courthouse, Hebron

TEMPLES OF JUSTICE   After fire destroyed the original Thayer County Courthouse in
Hebron, a new one was built in 1902. Left: Geneva's Fillmore County Courthouse was built in 1894.
A local man still climbs the narrow stairway up the tower to keep the clock working.

THE POWER OF WATER

North of Ayr, workers dammed the Little Blue River in 1893 to create Crystal Lake so they could harvest ice in the winter. Refrigeration ended the business in the 1920s; now the lake is a recreation area. Right: Champion Mill, near Nebraska's southwest corner, is the oldest functioning water-powered mill in the state. Built in the 1880s, it burned and was rebuilt in the 1890s. It is a state historical park.

Champion Mill, Chase County

Kearney Canal, on campus of University of Nebraska-Kearney

KEARNEY CANAL
Hydropower came to Kearney
in the 1880s, powering newfangled electric light bulbs
and Nebraska's first electric
trolleys.

CALAMUS LAKE

Today Calamus Lake
exists as an irrigation
supply reservoir and state
recreation area, but the
valley has been inhabited
for at least 3,000 years.

Calamus Reservoir, Loup County

North Star School, Red Cloud

Mallalieu University, Bartley

HIGHER EDUCATION

Across the state, schools and colleges sprouted from local initiative. Like the towns
themselves, some survived and some didn't.
Left to Right: An old country school north
of Cowles has been moved to Red Cloud.
Bartley's Methodist Church is built from
bricks intended for Mallalieu University,
which closed before its first permanent
building was completed. Peru State College
is Nebraska's oldest state-funded college.
Page 110-111: Wayne State College began in
1891 as Nebraska Normal College, a private
institution dedicated to teacher education.

Peru State College, Peru

Wayne State College, Wayne

U.S. Highway 281, Holt County

HIGHWAYS

An abandoned section of U.S. Highway 281 begins south of O'Neill. It was paved 1929-1930. Right: Looking north toward Cozad on State Highway 21. The road follows the 100th Meridian, which some say marks the approximate boundary between humid East and arid West.

100th Meridian, Dawson County

Spring Valley Park, Rock County

Sam Bass and the Big Springs Robbery, Deuel County

Highway Oases

The train is safe today, but in 1877
outlaw Sam Bass and his gang
made off with $60,000 in gold in
Nebraska's biggest train robbery.
Today a park in Big Springs is a
pleasant stop for I-80 travelers.
Left: Near the town of Newport in
1938, a local couple established
what's thought to be Nebraska's
first roadside rest area, now known
as Spring Valley Park.

Atlanta P.O.W. Camp, Phelps County

REMNANTS OF WAR An old chimney in Atlanta is one of the few physical traces of what was once a large camp for German prisoners during World War II. Right: Ruins of the World War I potash boomtown are still visible along Highway 2 near the Sandhills village of Antioch.

Antioch Potash Boomtown, Sheridan County

Andrew Jackson Higgins Memorial, Columbus

Fort Robinson P.O.W. Camp, Dawes County

FIGHTING THE WAR   A prisoner of war camp was built at Fort Robinson in 1943. Left: Columbus native Andrew Jackson Higgins is honored for designing a ship-to-shore landing craft used from D-Day through the Vietnam War. Page 120-121: Heartland of America Park is part of the original Omaha town site, and was once a warehouse district.

Heartland of America Park, Omaha

First National Bank Tower, Omaha

St. Paul, Howard County

EPILOGUE

Our story comes to a close, but the larger story of Nebraska and its people goes on. We look at past and present and wonder, "What's the next chapter?"

BEFORE NEBRASKA TERRITORY was officially opened to settlement, Peter Sarpy ran a little trading post at a place along the Missouri River called Bellevue. Among the many stories of Sarpy is one that appeared in an 1882 state history. It is attributed to J. Sterling Morton, a Nebraska pioneer and founder of Arbor Day. Morton's tale has the markings of Victorian-era fiction, but seems appropriate here nevertheless.

In Bellevue one day, Morton noticed that Sarpy was wearing a diamond on his lapel. Sarpy explained that it had belonged to his mother. During a visit home to St. Louis, Sarpy's brother had told him that the growing city needed the ground where their mother was buried. They dug up her coffin and moved it to a new graveyard. But Sarpy could not resist looking inside, and discovered the diamond his mother used to wear. He kept it as a memento of her.

Sarpy knew that "not many years will come and go before I, too, will be called to another life in another world. And then these fertile lands, these vast plains will have been settled up, and somewhere in this Missouri Valley, perhaps in sight of

Above: St. Paul native Grover Cleveland Alexander might take issue with the "Batting 1000" slogan. The legendary pitcher preferred to keep batting averages low. Left: Omaha's First National Bank Tower.

I-80, Kimball County

where we now stand, a great city will have been builded up, and there will ever and ever go up hence a hum of contented industry. Then I may have been in my grave many years, and with me will have rested in darkness this gem."

Because Sarpy had no children, he warned Morton that someday men might come to him, saying, "the city needs room, and you must take his old bones away." He advised Morton to open his coffin, take the diamond and wear it, and to be buried with it himself. But, he warned, some day Morton's sons would have to move his bones, too. "I tell you, sir, this cry for 'Room! more room!' for the living... will never, never cease!"

Since Sarpy's time, Nebraska has become a curious mixture of urban and rural elements. Nebraska is urban: Today, more than half of Nebraskans live in the state's two largest cities. Only a small minority still work the farms and ranches for which the state is traditionally known.

Nebraska is rural: Outside Omaha and Lincoln, Nebraska remains a place of small towns and sparsely-populated countryside.

Can Nebraska's cities retain their "Nebraska-ness," or is there something inevitable about urban sprawl and homogenization? Can Nebraska's small towns remain viable as full-fledged communities as their founders envisioned?

Nebraska's historic places and their stories don't promise success. What they say is that others have pursued their particular visions here, and that someone found that pursuit worth remembering.

Whether the story of the diamond originated with Sarpy or not, it speaks of the difficulty of reconciling pioneers' contradictory wishes – the desire to found cities, and the equal longing to hold onto the natural places they loved and the small communities where they felt at home. After all these years, Nebraska still has the opportunity to realize both wishes.

State Capitol, Lincoln

EAST AND WEST
Nebraska State Capitol in Lincoln.
Left: I-80 in Kimball County, near Nebraska's western boundary.

South 24th, Omaha

Arcadia parade, Valley County

CITY AND TOWN

Veterans form the color
guard at a parade in Arcadia.
Left: Downtown "South O"
bustles with shoppers along
South 24th Street in Omaha.

Johnson Lake, Gosper and Dawson Counties

Land and Water

Built for irrigation, Johnson Lake has become a popular recreation site. Page 130-131: Lewis and Clark Lake. Page 132-133: Republican River, where a devastaing flood killed 110 people in 1935. Page 134-135: Looking east through Mitchell Pass, with Highway 92 on the right and scars of the Oregon Trail on the left. Page 136-137: Chimney Rock in Morrill County. Page 138-139: Near Mullen in the Sandhills.

Lewis and Clark Lake, Knox County

Republican River

Mitchell Pass, Scotts Bluff County

Chimney Rock, Morrill County

Sandhills, near Mullen

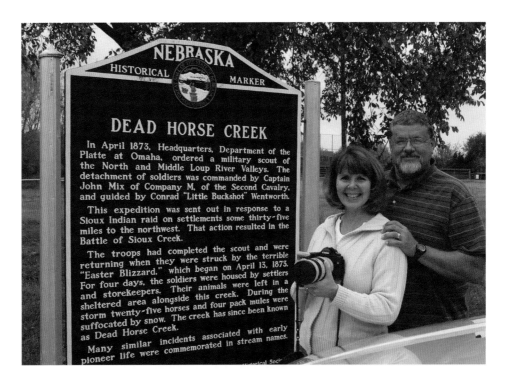

WE URGE YOU TO CONSIDER THE 400-PLUS HISTORICAL MARKERS and other historical sites across Nebraska as an open invitation to get off the highway. Explore Nebraska's unique and unexpected landscapes and visit its welcoming communities. You'll see the state and its history from an exciting new perspective.

We wish to thank the Nebraska State Historical Society, their local chapters and others for keeping these snippets of Nebraska's history close at hand. Also, thank you to Chris Amundson, Dave Bristow, Camille Kirchhoff, Anthony Kuhlman and the rest of the staff at *Nebraska Life* for sharing our vision for this book. Thanks especially to our parents, Glenn and Emily Petersen and Ted and the late Fran Olson, for planting the seeds of exploration in us as kids on those long, leisurely afternoon drives with the family.

– Steve and Bobbi Olson

Discover more about Nebraska
with *Nebraska Life Magazine*

After 10 years, we're still amazed by the variety of stories that we find. One day we're photographing rock-and-roll musicians in Omaha's Sokol Hall. The next day we're riding a horse at a branding at a Sandhills ranch. We've written about danger and heroism during western Nebraska wildfires, about the simple joy of picking wild asparagus in the spring, and about the father-son bond formed on game day at Memorial Stadium.

What have we learned about life in Nebraska?
We'll say this much: There's always more to discover.

1 year (6 issues) • $21 2 years (12 issues) • $38
To order today call or visit our website.

800-777-6159 • www.NebraskaLife.com
Already a Subscriber? Share the Good Life with a Friend – Give a Gift Subscription!

The Magazine That Explores Nebraska

202 Norfolk Avenue • PO Box 819 • Norfolk, NE 68702

Olson, Bobbi and Steve
   Marking Time: Nebraska's Historic Places/Bobbi and Steve Olson
   Includes index

ISBN: 978-0-9789364-2-6
Manufactured in the United States of America
First Edition/First Printing November 2007

Published by

NEBRASKA LIFE

Nebraska Life Publishing
202 West Norfolk Avenue
PO Box 819
Norfolk, NE 68702-0819
USA

Publisher/President: Christopher Amundson
Vice President: Angela Amundson

Text by David L. Bristow
Book design by Camille Kirchhoff
Additional design by Anthony Kuhlmann

To buy books in quantity for corporate use or incentives, call 800-777-6159 or email premiums@NebraskaLife.com

Visit us online www.NebraskaLife.com

Cover: Fort Niobrara in Cherry County
Inset Back Cover: Fort Atkinson in Washington County